In the Beginning

Illustrations by
Bent L. Hanson and Flemming Walsoe

Calligraphy by
Faith Scarborough

Copyright 1986, Paul C. Brownlow
ISBN: 0-915720-22-1

Quotations from The Holy Bible,
New International Version.
Copyright 1978 New York International Bible Society.
Used by permission.

Brownlow Publishing Company, Inc.
6309 Airport Freeway, Fort Worth, Texas 76117

In the Beginning

The story of creation as told in the book of Genesis.

BROWNLOW PUBLISHING COMPANY, INC.

FORT WORTH, TEXAS

*In the beginning
God created
the heavens and
the earth. Now
the earth was
formless and
empty,
darkness was
over the surface
of the deep…*

... and the Spirit of God was hovering over the waters.

And God said, "Let there be light," and there was light.

*God saw that
the light
was good, and
he separated
the light from
the darkness.
God called
the light "day"
and
the darkness he
called "night."*

And there was evening, and there was morning—the first day.

And God said, "Let there be
an expanse between the
waters to separate water from
water." So God made
the expanse and separated
the water under the expanse
from the water above it.
And it was so. God
called the expanse
"sky."

And there was evening, and there was morning —the second day.

And God said, "Let the water under the sky be gathered to one place, and let dry ground appear." And it was so.

16

God called
the dry
ground "land"…

… and the
gathered waters
he called "seas."
And God saw
that it was
good.

Then God said, "Let the land produce vegetation: seed-bearing plants and trees on the land that bear fruit with seed in it, according to their various kinds." And it was so.

The land produced vegetation: plants bearing seed according to their kinds and trees bearing fruit with seed in it according to their kinds.

And God saw that it was good.

*And there
was evening,
and there
was morning
—the third day.*

And God said, "Let there be lights in the expanse of the sky to separate the day from the night, and let them serve as signs to mark seasons and days and years, and let them be lights in the expanse of the sky to give light on the earth." *And it was so.*

*God made two
great lights—
the greater light
to govern the day
and the lesser light
to govern the night.
He also made the stars.
God set them in
the expanse of
the sky to give light on
the earth, to govern
the day and the night, and
to separate light from
darkness. And God saw
that it was good.*

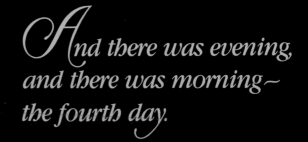

And there was evening, and there was morning~ the fourth day.

And God said, "Let the water teem with living creatures…

32

...and let birds fly above the earth across the expanse of the sky."

So God created the great creatures of the sea and every living and moving thing with which the water teems, according to their kinds…

*...and every
winged bird
according to
its kind.*

*And God saw
that it was good.*

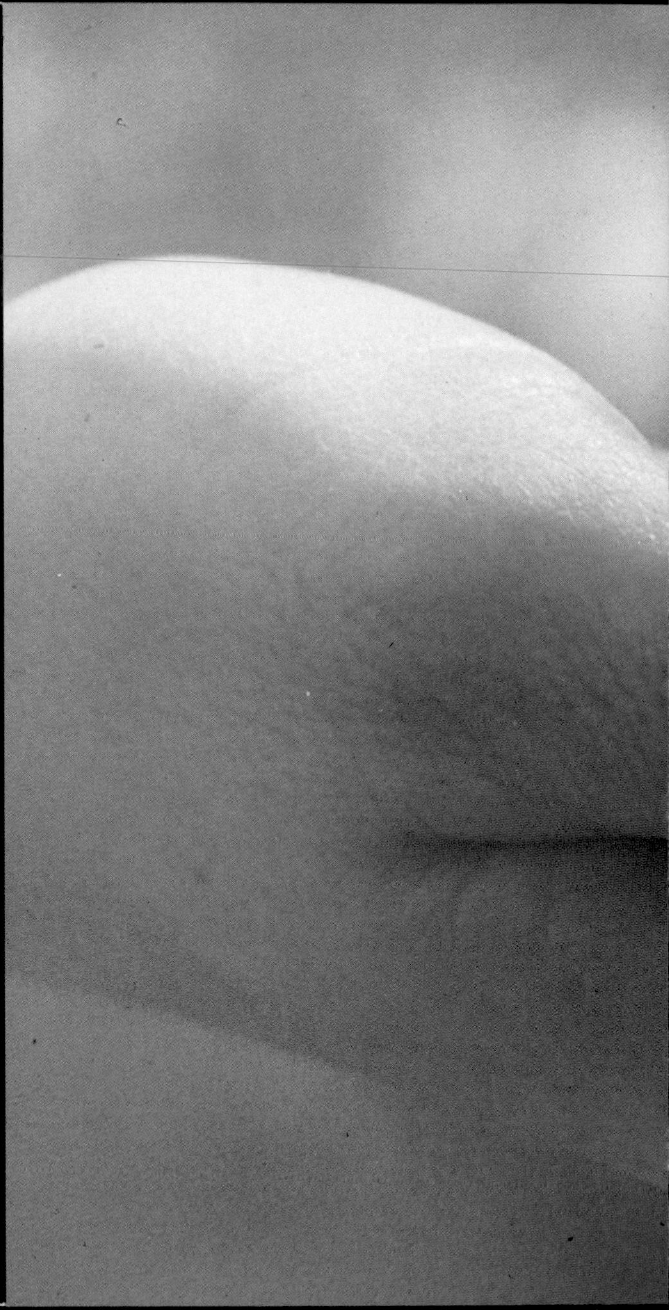

*God blessed
them and
said, "Be fruitful
and increase
in number and fill
the water in the
seas, and let the
birds increase on
the earth."*

And there was evening, and there was morning —the fifth day.

And God said, "Let the
land produce living creatures
according to their kinds…

*…livestock,
creatures that
move along the
ground, and wild
animals, each
according to
its kind."
And it was so.*

God made the wild animals according to their kinds, the livestock according to their kinds, and all the creatures that move along the ground according to their kinds.

And
God saw that it
was good.

Then God said, "Let us make man in our image, in our likeness, and let them rule over the fish of the sea and the birds of the air, over the livestock, over all the earth, and over all the creatures that move along the ground."

So God created man in his own image, in the image of God he created him; male and female he created them.

God blessed them and said to them, "Be fruitful and increase in number; fill the earth and subdue it. Rule over the fish of the sea and the birds of the air and over every living creature that moves on the ground."

Then God said, "I give you every seed-bearing plant on the face of the whole earth and every tree that has fruit with seed in it. They will be yours for food.

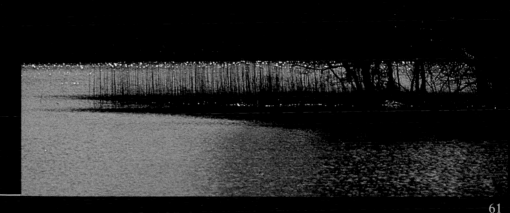

*And to all the beasts of
the earth and all the birds
of the air and all the
creatures that move on the
ground—everything that has
the breath of life in it—I give
every green plant for food."
And it was so.*

God saw all that he had made, and it was very good.

And there was evening,
and there was morning
—the sixth day.

Thus the heavens and the earth were completed in all their vast array. By the seventh day God had finished the work he had been doing.

PHOTOS BY:	PAGE:
Bent L. Hansen:	Cover, 4, 7, 9, 11, 13, 14, 23, 29, 30, 31, 32, 33, 36, 37B, 43B, 45, 49, 51, 52, 53, 55, 56, 58, 60, 62, 65, 66.
Flemming Walsøe:	5, 6, 8, 16, 18, 19, 20, 22, 24, 25, 27, 35, 37A, 38, 39, 42, 43A, 46, 47, 50, 59, 61, 63.
Robert Cushman Hayes:	12, 34, 41.
H. von Haeseler:	15.
Jørgen Vium Olesen:	17.